Leaves of Fall

Leaves of Fall

Amanjeet K. Sungha

RUPA

Published by
Rupa Publications India Pvt. Ltd 2021
7/16, Ansari Road, Daryaganj
New Delhi 110002

Sales Centres:
Allahabad Bengaluru Chennai
Hyderabad Jaipur Kathmandu
Kolkata Mumbai

Text and illustrations copyright © Amanjeet K. Sungha 2021
Illustration by: Milan Jain

The views and opinions expressed in this book are the author's own and the facts are as reported by her which have been verified to the extent possible, and the publishers are not in any way liable for the same.

All rights reserved.
No part of this publication may be reproduced, transmitted, or stored in a retrieval system, in any form or by any means, electronic, mechanical, photocopying, recording or otherwise, without the prior permission of the publisher.

ISBN: 978-93-5333-950-0

First impression 2021

10 9 8 7 6 5 4 3 2 1

Printed at Parksons Graphics Pvt. Ltd, Mumbai

The moral right of the author has been asserted.

This book is sold subject to the condition that it shall not, by way of trade or otherwise, be lent, resold, hired out, or otherwise circulated, without the publisher's prior consent, in any form of binding or cover other than that in which it is published.

For Mom, Dad and you
and the leaves

Contents

OF HOPE

1.	A Belief is Born	3
2.	Light of Love	5
3.	Yearnings of a Sky	6
4.	When Hope Speaks	7
5.	An Ode to a Thought	8
6.	Tiny Hole of Hope	9
7.	The Sea Sings	11
8.	A Prayer Whispers	13
9.	My Sky	14
10.	An Ode to a Pond	17
11.	When Faith Speaks	19
12.	Iron Will of Souls	20
13.	An Ode to a Journey	21
14.	In a Search	22
15.	He Falls	23
16.	A Road Diverges	25
17.	A Song of Success	27

OF LIFE

18.	Life, I Am	31
19.	Is It Pain or Longing?	32
20.	Where Mercy Doesn't Reach	33
21.	Silence	35
22.	Of Avarice	36
23.	Half Lives	39
24.	The Day Dies	41
25.	The Same Place Again	42
26.	When Life Echoes	44
27.	A Stranded River	45

28. A Smile	46
29. An Ode to Joy	48
30. Of Memories	51
31. On Silence	52
32. The Mind Crumbles	53
33. She Died	55
34. We Almost Never Feel	56
35. Scarred Dreams	57
36. My Body Is to Die	58
37. The Walls I Live In	59
38. The Summer of Sorrow	60
39. Of Questions	62
40. The City of My Gods	63

OF LOSS

41. A Lost Companion	67
42. The Truth Comes in Pieces	69
43. A Lost Season	71
44. It's Been a While	72
45. The Shades of a Memory	73
46. The Fissures of Fortune	74
47. Looking for You	75
48. In Betrayal	77
49. The Notes of a Faithless	78
50. He Languishes	79
51. Painted Dreams	81
52. The Beleaguered Tales	83
53. Cacophony of a Muted Dream	84
54. In Memory of a Man	85
55. Of Benefactors	86

OF LOVE

56. Of a Moon	91
57. Love's Wine	92

58. Love's Feather — 93
59. You and I — 94
60. Your Light upon Me — 96
61. He Walks by Me — 97
62. Conjugal in Faith — 98
63. Love's Song — 99
64. Leaves Sing — 101
65. I Search for You — 103
66. Ode to Innocence — 105

OF HER

67. Her Silence — 109
68. She Weaves a Cloth — 111
69. She Sees Beauty — 112
70. I am a Bird — 113
71. She Smiles — 114
72. The Light of a Woman — 115
73. A Broken Leaf — 116
74. Is It Mine? — 117
75. She Wears a Thin Smile — 119
76. Forever My Credence — 121
77. In a Woman Like You — 123
78. The Girl Stands — 124
79. A Birth Unwanted — 127
80. A Leaf of Fall — 128
81. She Walks Alone — 129
82. Of Different Women — 131
83. Of Joyful Cage — 132
84. Of Subjugation — 135
85. She is Silent, Forevermore — 137
86. Of Dreams of Freedom — 138
87. To a Father, from Daughter — 141

OF HOPE

Wish I was a bird, with feathers of joy,
With wind on my wings.
Mountains as abodes on my lovely swings,
I would build a nest of lovely leaves.
With a home in the midst of shades,
that love weaves.

A Belief is Born

In the dark of this night
a light shines through,
And somewhere inside me
a belief is born.

That without pain
life would be too meaningless,
Without these tired feet
there wouldn't be a joy in the walk.

When sands of oceans were
adrift with their waters,
The shores held on
but no one saw their torment.

I had risen through the words from
under the sunken thoughts,
And without these aching letters
earth wouldn't remember my name.

Light of Love

The morning sun comes with a promise of shine,
And graces its mother earth divine,
Rays of hope peep through the trees,
As they spread in morning breeze,
The leaves turn into golden green,
A panorama spreads on a natural screen,
Think of the sun as light of love,
It spreads the message like a golden dove,
All get its love in equal measure,
That's plenty in nature's treasure.

Yearnings of a Sky

In this cold rainy night, I sit in my bed
with a blanket that covers me half,
The pillow comforts my head with its softness
Yet a hardness aches in my head.

I stare out of the window,
The clouds are in a rush of happy urgency
and the moon is quietly still.

The wind gushes in suddenly
and strays the clouds from their path
to their home.

The moon stays still,
I sit passive,
My feet are cold and my head still aches.

I feel a constant yearning
of the bearers of the sky
they call heaven.

When Hope Speaks

Hope speaks to the soul of the forsaken,
And inflicts the passionate with a strength ,
The sound of the universe reassures,
That you are not alone here.

If you won't rise up,
Whose journey would they write about,
If you won't speak
whose story would they say.

Where would hope's spring fall
If you won't look up,
And how would light find her path
If you won't show the way.

And as you glow in this darkness tonight,
The earth shall gather the streams of her life,
And fairies will rejuvenate the hills with their stories,
That without you,
This hope too would die.

An Ode to a Thought

I am a thought
that wanders carelessly
through the universe.
When a bright ray of
sun crosses my window,
I spread manifold
and manifest in the
minds of the men.
When a creaking sound
of a door disturbs my
concentration, I quietly hide
in the darkness behind and lay there
to find the grease of imagination
that'll move me.
I am undone by the memory,
I am often lying wasted,
But I am in your mind,
A God's particle unutilized.

Tiny Hole of Hope

Hope is looking at me,
I look in its eyes,
It wants me to know
the path it travels each day.

How it reaches the beleaguered soul
holding firm in winds that shake,
Rowing through the storm
while everything gives up to the doom.

It takes dive in the darkest cave
of the gloomiest thoughts,
And sits there, unheard to all,
And creates a tiny hole of hope.

The black clouds of doubt hide it,
And the rain of fear drowns it in,
And it survives the onslaught
of human despair, of frailty.

I want to give away,
Look away,
But it watches me,
Unworried of my hopelessness.

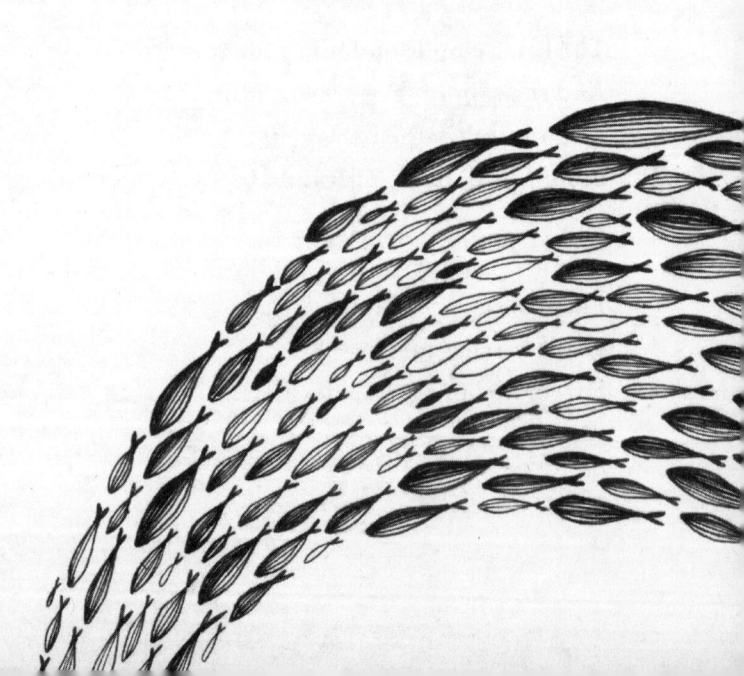

The Sea Sings

The sea sings
in its blueness,
The songs it tells
rest on its waves
and travel to our heart.

Its bosom hides the secrets
of its depths,
Yet the sea doesn't lie
to those who truly seek it.
It speaks to them
of its creatures and the music
in a language of stillness.

The sea is dark and white,
It's blue and red
as the eye wants to see it.
Who knows the tales
of its stormy nights,
And who could fathom
the beauty of its calm!

A boatman sails on
battling with its flow,
Blind to what a sea holds

he seeks a part of its bounty.
And the benevolent sea
smiles with him
and gives him life.

A Prayer Whispers

The wind shakes leaves into madness of a song,
A bird somewhere chirps along,
And grasshoppers and crickets all going gong,
A train far away beeps into rhymes,
And stars of the night are having sparkling times,
A moon that borrows her charms from the sun
awaits her kiss that's a thousand miles run,
Amidst all songs of joy and spark,
Somewhere a prayer whispers in the dark.

My Sky

In the moonlight, in the dark, this blue sky floats,
A constant to all weathers and seasons,
Stars couldn't hide it behind their shine
and moon couldn't have lived without it.

It features the tales I weave alone, unshared,
    un-shaded, untended,
I build replicas on it and destroy them while they churn
    my soul inside,
In this sky, I can't discern a difference of one star from
    the other and one shape from another,
Something I am good at seeing in humans.

It's a starry sky located above my hearth, beaming above
    my sorrows,
And sadness of it all, it doesn't care to lose its shimmer,
Maybe it's teaching me something I can't learn.

This sky has seen the universe expanding in rage,
When oceans couldn't douse the fires of burning
    meteors, it watched as a silent observer, unperturbed,
Neither in joy, nor in sadness,

While I try to time the existence of what lies above,
I find a companion who is a constant to me, my own,
It stays constant in expanse and gives me the space I
    couldn't find among humans.

An Ode to a Pond

I see a pond in the midst of trees,
With its muddy edges full of fallen leaves,
I look in the water and it has different shades,
Somewhere green, somewhere dark,
Somewhere it all fades.

I see reflections so varied and pure,
In the tiny pond which is nobody's eye's cynosure,
I see in it the image of heaven and its colours,
White clouds drape
blue Cinderella into covers.

Trees look deep in the mirror bestowed,
I think God's given them a special abode,
Wonder what trees talk to this pond!
To its calm stillness and its cool warmth,
They must thank him for this wonderful bond.

This pond stays there,
All unnoticed,
It brims with life when rains unleash,
Sleeping alone when rain is gone
it's sick and yellow, as if jaundiced.

This pond does have hope
to give to others,
A thirsty sparrow gets water from its womb,
A man sits here to find his image,
And lonely heart finds a solace, I assume.

When Faith Speaks

Faith speaks, faith creaks,
Faith is a season of myriad colours,
Faith is a hope of hopeless lovers.

A thousand mercenaries wave their flag,
An old ascetic sits with beads in his bag,
Wonder if faith is understood,
And a million crusaders would swag their hood.

Where will I go, hither or ho?
I would sit just here, lo!
I would not waiver,
I am taught in traditions great,
I would un-swirl the tides of hate.

I would conjure the spells of love,
I would unfold the feathers of dove,
May it flies to holy-unholy lands,
Puts its colours on faithful hands,
And faith would blend,
But not of the hawkish trend.

Iron Will of Souls

The forest of hope beckons,
Yet a shade of doubt persists,
It ignites the flame of toil,
And leads the chariots of victory!

The seasons of defeat wait,
Yet not unknown to them,
To weather the storms of desire,
Rows of conjured gods stand!

To stay still in the turbulence,
The boats of iron weren't enough,
Clouds of rain wander in the sky,
And the iron will of souls roar!

An Ode to a Journey

lone journeys are their own pilgrims
where mortals spin around unaware,
A silent traveller walks with a silent road,
A lonely heart listens to the songs

of some shadows that travel along,
Only for seconds, sometimes even less,
Then night falls and stars accompany,
But only so to say,
They are in their own journey too.

Cycle of life plays mischief and ruins a perfect company,
But mountains of grass were only to be lifted,
Not by happy shoulders,
But by strength of a seed's sojourn.

As the hours waive their adieu,
Time clocks a journey unknown,
I sum up miles squandered, motionless,
Eyes are stuck, mind is blind.

And in the vicinity of times, as stars talk today,
I know I have a mile still in stride,
Not exactly to reach somewhere
but to make up the lost distance.

In a Search

A man knocks on a door,
What does he seek?
A refuge for a bruised body?
Or kindness for an agonized soul?
Or to rendezvous with the less ordinary?

What makes him knock
on the strangest door in the city?
A vague belief
to hear a decent voice?
Or a guile to share a mean fruit of someone's life?

Will he hear from behind that shut door?
Or the voice behind is shut forever?
Is he unwelcome here?
Is the man inside bereaved of faith?

He looks up to the sky,
He does not see any light,
He turns his back on the door,
And moves on,
To look for another door.

He Falls

In a world of hate,
He looks for a place to walk free,
As he struggles to find his way,
Feet stumble on the reflections of anger,
And he falls.

As he gets to his feet again,
He hears the cry of a child unloved,
And he knows he is among depraved,
And his feet shiver again.

He looks around,
The light of the day deprived of life stares at him,
He knows eyes won't delight anymore, anywhere,
And yet again, something reminds him of hope.

Perhaps a face of child playing with water nearby,
A blaze of fire passes through the heart of the earth and
    dies,
Perhaps there's another hope he may look for,
And he may walk free.

A Road Diverges

A road diverges and merges with another road,
Well it knows it's carrying some load.

Humans walk on in various styles
Some for home, some go places and some exiles,
A few gain distance and many miss many a miles.

Some succeed, some are defeated,
This road watches them all unperturbed.

Wailing like child, some sit aside,
Twisting tornadoes, some are defeating a tide.

Hazy storms kill many in an oblivion's grind,
Toil through whirling winds is many a vigorous mind.

Free as birds with spirit delight,
Some find zenith, some blight.

Floodlights on the sides have some significance,
Some are blinded by the glow,
Sure it makes many reach magnificence.

Road diverges not just once,
That's its glory, that's the essence.

Where we go, what happens indeed,
That's all guaranteed in our creed,
And sure this road won't be the lead.

A Song of Success

People say its possible, people say its not,
Everyone is here for a long shot;
What's in a possibility?

Miles achieved, may shadow your tiny walks,
A sparrow maybe tiny for the mighty hawks;
What's in the size?

Crimson red may diminish white's glory,
Yet everyone is their own story,
Write it well.

You may not reach moons,
May not find the star,
Just don't lose the strings of your guitar.

OF LIFE

A flower lives for a while,
A short life,
A beautiful life,
She withers, perhaps she cries,
Her time on earth is small, she leaves in the twinkle of an eye.

Life, I Am

Dripping in rays of light
I know I am a mist that cools,
Soothing like a feather's touch
I know when a heart needs me as much.

If I hurt like a woodcutter's axe,
Forgive me; I give the shape that has to be,
When in trench a bugle sorrows
if it rains stars, I would borrow.

Sudden flights to no where may carry me afar,
It's just the way the journey was carved,
Sometimes I'll wander in joys of mundane,
Well, I may fail you without a gain.

Some patterns give me an existence,
I am however a wandering persistence,
I muddle in joys and tears,
Sometimes pious, sometimes of sin,
But I can't get back to my own origin.

Is It Pain or Longing?

I am walking with life,
She laughs at my middle name,
Is it pain or longing?

A man wrought with pain
buried himself in the sand,
Shores betrayed soon when waters hit them,
Sand was washed away
and he was left un-bared.

Could he hide?
Like a shadow it follows him,
Just like shadows wane, it too flows
in tears at night, and return.

It's not silent like a shadow,
It carries a story in its womb
and it talks to him
in a voice of his own.

Where Mercy Doesn't Reach

I know where mercy doesn't reach,
Where god fails to remember,
Through the windows, silently, they await him,
The rust of pain doesn't wash, not just with brush of palms.

Hands join and hearts stay crossed,
In the untidy springs of life, prayers lay waste,
Like rains in winter, unwelcomed,
And lips shiver in a hope, lost.

And grains of life hold on,
Their existence is as tiny as their hope,
Life falls, like sand slips from hands,
It's hard to grab and light in its fall.

They still stay awake, counting the threads of their beads,
As it all lasts, some soul gives way,
The rains did come,
The showers of mercy didn't pour for him.

Silence

A dim flicker of light,
It falls on the shadow of the men,
It's a fire conceived in quiet.

In the deep dry woods,
It's a wish of the sound
to lie buried, reluctant.

It's a wall that surrounds
without a feeling, unmoved,
It's a wall that bounds, forever,
For it contains it, in solitude.

It's a glance into the closed eyes,
Where the deep voice finds itself
uncontained, by a burrough like
a frenzied beat.

Like a light of star, un-borrowed
it exists for itself, or for us,
When all lays silent
It's what holds on.

Of Avarice

I hear the noises
of vanity
grow strong in my mind,
and wayward,
I follow.

I listen to the voice
of avarice unprecedented
take me over,
And I yearn for more
of it.

I see the face
of my hunger
on me, in my bright attire,
And my loaded hands
seek fruits forbidden.

I watch the sky
of blue
change its hue to grey,
With clouds of covetous
unbridled.

The dying light in me
struggles in vain
to survive
the lightlessness
of redundance.

Half Lives

In the middle of this quiet night
there are thoughts of my half-lived life,
My poor life,
My thoughts languish in mis-designed circles of my mind
which never meant to give me any meaning,
And they linger.

Think of all men,
Men of other life mock the world of half lives
like mine,
While I listen to their scorn on my existence
I wonder at their half life,
And my thoughts fight a battle with me.

Where do they bring that cacophony of hatred from?
Where did they forget the symphony of belief?
Why do I care to listen to it all?
It's the miraculous game of odds they play,
And some lose and some lose more,
And I stay silent.

In the passing shadow of each day,
The belief of my unnourished soul is put to a daring test,

And all it sees is a hollow figure of men,
Not meant to live beyond frivolous,
Riddled with an unclamped mischief,
Filled with poverty of soul, of half lives.

The Day Dies

I stay still
and the day moves on,
The sunlight falls in the corners
of the silent room
and then wane away.

The shadows enter through
the leaves of a tree adjacent to window,
And a bird chirps on,
Out of habit,
With no purpose.

The silence eases in,
It breaks the noise of this day,
The day is dying again, I see,
Without an endeavour,
Without a fight to live.

The Same Place Again

I stay up in the nights
with eyes half closed,
I watch the stars
barely visible in cover of this cloudy city,
An image of a giant tree stares at me.

A thought would hold on for a while,
Then just pass as it never was,
Like some things that could only hold you
until a slight move of the eyes
and then are lost in dark edges of their existence,

The stars seem to be too distant now
unlike the stars of that night of my childhood,
Ah! the stars looked so bright then,
Their light was descending to illuminate my soul,
A soul unaware of what it meant to burn.

I would watch them
with thoughts comforted by their light,
And tiny bright eyes were busy
drawing, redrawing the marvel
in the universe of the stars.

The stars of tonight seem to move away
yet leaving a tail of light,
I might trace them
and maybe, when I go back to the same place again,
I will find them just there,
Unpersuaded,
By the times that swayed me away.

When Life Echoes

It's a silent day with lots of noise,
The usual shimmer of life,
The usual uneasiness,
And perhaps little more.

I hear the sound of love
longing somewhere
in an eternal quest,
In a wait.

The sun sweeps the earth,
And it heats up,
Like the emotions inside me
disquieting the peace outside.

Life sits in a corner
Bestowed with herself,
She looks at me with hope
and I wander into a dream.

Could I smile with her?
Or play to her rhythm?
I just sit quiet
and hear her echo.

A Stranded River

These waves have caught my sight,
They seem confused,
They are moving hither and thither like a lost traveller,
The waves besides them are strong in their gait,
And swell by the pride in their direction.

My waves are in motionless silence,
With quiet stones as their companions,
Why do they seem so lost?
Is it the lost direction or lost passion for it?
Could it be that shallowness beneath them killed their
    stride?

And confused they dwell,
Hitting the shores without a noise,
The sound of river is passing them by,
And birds in flock fly past along the river
with an occasional drift on their bosom.

These waves are a stranded river, deserted in their path,
Still not alone I believe they are,
Light of the sky still shine on them,
A man still looks at them with hope,
And the feet feel warm with their touch still.

A Smile

A smile talks to him
And asks his name,
'I am stranger to her
for so long,' he thinks,
'And yet she smiles at me
like my own.'

She is vigorous,
Disarming
and beautiful,
All in a wondrous chord,
'I would follow her,' he thinks,
Only to fail.

She is the dawn
he wants to wake into,
She is the maiden
of joy,
And in her reflection
he wants to live, forever.

But closer he looks,
She broods too,
For the half smiles,
Lost zest,

For wooden beliefs
and forgotten faces.

She tells him a story
of a man
who never smiled,
And then he died!
And how she longed
for once to
have him smile!

An Ode to Joy

Joy speaks
silently,
It's noisy occasionally,
Mostly it flows
through the chambers of our hearts,
Unknown.

Like a breezy drizzle on earth
it soothes,
Sometimes it stays on
echoing through us,
Smiling and waving
to life forever.

Sometimes it visits
like a passing second,
In a momentary laugh,
In a quiet smile,
Jostling with us through our moments
lived in grief.

While it lasts briefly or more,
It spreads itself,
Creates a symphony of itself,

Ever it lasts,
It breaths with that quiet room
and it knows it was happy once.

Of Memories

Times float in silence,
And memories call me back,
They live on in me,
Like a lake trapped in a valley,
Frozen with its winters,
They reverberate through me
and torment me
whenever I take their name.

On Silence

You listen to the agony of a loss
And to the tale of a wanderer,
You talk to the flowing waters
And to the grieving hearts,
You are the bliss of the solitude
And of a silent mind,
You speak in the silent corner of a room
And in the creaking sounds of old doors,
You smile in the laughter of the trees
And in the flutter of the dancing leaves,
You sing in the snowy mountains
And in the meandering rivers,
When eyes look for solace of tears
You silently accompany them,
You live in the broken arches of a home
And in the silent sighs of a woman,
You echo in the fields ravaged with war
And in the roads deserted by men,
You are the soul of the unspoken
And music of the unsaid.

The Mind Crumbles

Shapes move seemlessly
on the wooden edges of my thoughts,
A few hit the roofs of my mind
like a lightning strikes the earth
and fades just as fast.

Some crawl up slow and strike deep of the rough
like a woodpecker's peck,
Never failing to rake the hidden
echo as they strike,
Even in retreat
deep cracks in me are revealed that
unravel a careful decorated sprawl of human.

Savouring brilliance of their mammoth,
Ceilings of my mind crumble with their giant
    unfathomed vanity,
My carefully decorated house gets tired and
wary of being a nice host.

The colours on my walls faint,
A soul fortified gives way, the walls age,
As all the shapes wither, withering with the shapes
is my reticent timeless rage.

She Died

The story has died today,
She had to die,
She spoke the truth,
She rose to the ruth,
She died of her will,
No one ever really kill!

We Almost Never Feel

There is a joy in an ailing heart
just as quiet as a thin layer of wind on our face
that we almost never feel.

There is laughter in sorrow too
just as unwanted as crackle to the ears
of the leaves that are crushed under our feet.

There is a voice in the silence
like the whispers of the birds that no one cares to recall.

There is music in the tears,
It flows like mist on leaves, never adorned.

A smile is hidden in melancholy
like a flower fallen off its branch, invisible on earth.

There is a life in the shires of death
almost as quiet as the sound of a man in the valley.

Scarred Dreams

The day opens up
with wealth of its hours,
He wakes up to the promise of a dream,
And yet again the day ends,
In noise,
In haste,
Poorer than yesterday.

He stays awake long after the dark,
The night has put a halt, timidly,
To the moving ambitions around him,
In a quiet solace
he enriches,
But his dream lays waste with him
and the day's shrill rings high in his ears.

His dreams don't dare come near him
when un-holiness of ambitions scream high,
As his mind withers
like a withering moon,
He is eternally scarred,
The curse of his ambitions, still he carries
and wane he must.

My Body Is to Die

My body is to die one day,
If I die in a memory that's my death.

Tears dry when eyes shut,
If I cry in fear that's my death.

Who doesn't mourn a demise,
If I mourn the life that's my death.

We don't see those who leave us,
If eyes lose hope that's my death.

Empty are spaces of those long gone,
If a place deserts me that's my death.

Shoulders elude in the walks of life,
If shoulders don't walk me that's my death.

A pyre of fire is my ultimate home,
If a fire leaves me that's my death.

Journey is all we share on this earth,
If I betray the path that's my death.

The Walls I Live In

I dwell in the walls of a prison,
Of hope and despair,
It's wintery cold
and pitched dark inside.

Seasons die in despair
but it watches me breathless, eternally,
Like the streams of endless flow,
With no bridges to cross
I still wait for my dawn.

Winter's bequeath to the season is
a spring on trees,
I await my spring too,
In the prison I
chose to be.

The Summer of Sorrow

I see the summer coming,
The moisture in the air
dampens the very spirit of me,
The summer of sorrow
hides inside me
and speaks
with misty eyes
of the broken moors.

The winter hadn't been mine,
The unkind wind
tore into the skin,
And gave me the chilling whispers,
Of disquiet,
Of cold,
Of the icy roads
slippery and dangerous.

The summer engulfs me,
Teething into my heart
with a blazing hot wind,
Burns me, torments me,
And I suffer,
I ask the earth for solace,
And she is quiet, quiet
as death.

Once an earthly joy on feet
now gives blisters,
I endure,
I am sure of the rain,
Which day would it be
when she knocks at my sky?
To water the parched mind!
To fill the chasm of the soul!

Of Questions

Is there anything un-happier than a sky
full of stars and nobody looks up to see?

Can a moon sing happily ever
when nobody comes to listen to her?

Won't grass weep mercilessly
when nobody feels her dew?

Would a blooming flower be forever silent
because nobody cared to caress her?

How silly is it for the rain to walk through black clouds
when no one dances in her path?

Why does a girl wait with eyes on the road
when she knows he has gone afar?

How sorrowful is a river that flows down the stream
without a bird flying along?

The City of My Gods

I sit here in this place, of nonchalant noises,
Hardly matters if I survive, or breathe,
But this place thrives, everyday beyond.

Tiny fragments of this place are stiller than I could've
    fathomed,
Where noises cut me short, shorter to my beliefs,
And winter of hope leaves me cold.

I try to see through the prism of its beliefs,
Could I see any sparkling light of a different hue?
And I see a painful ray, struggling for its path.

Could I find the formless benevolence of my holy gods?
While the rich chariots through, the gods of poor stare at
    hollow spaces,
And I look for a tiny crevice, where my spirit would meet
    her form.

OF LOSS

A leaf fell off its branch
And it cried
Nobody came to
Pick it up,
None adorned it ever,
It died without love.

A Lost Companion

My feet ache with this long walk,
My dreary body wants me to halt,
And as I gather my breath,
I see an old lady pass by.

A tiny figure folded in a robe of black,
Slightly bent, old age it seems,
And probably with all the life she had carried upon her
she doesn't look around at the life anymore.

She is scared to rise up the sidewalks,
It needs some strength to climb up and down
these faulty sidewalks,
She walks slow and fragile
on the edges of this road,
And I am still, something strikes inside me,
Pity or fear I couldn't decipher.

She stops a few steps away,
And as I would know, she is tired,
She sits on the sidewalk,
She knows she still has some miles
to walk alone.

And I wonder what she thinks,
Her eyes are dry of dried up dreams,
But life still seems to float in them
like a boat made of paper,
Sinking slowly as edges wither,
I try but I can't feel the ache of those feet,
Cold on earth, bereft of a companion.

The Truth Comes in Pieces

The darkness descended and he died,
He wasn't the man to live forever,
Hardened souls he laid siege on however
live on.

The God of uncertain terms!
Never to shy, easy on enchantments,
Did he arrive too early
or stayed too late?

The truth comes in pieces, through broken mirrors,
Through the ruthless untruths,
Reeking through the faithful and
tearing them apart.

Now he is buried
Unblessed!
Lying quietly,
Inside the tomb of a cold stone.

A Lost Season

A dream just went by me, in cold,
Here I cry for a shine-less gold,
Why did she send me alone?
What did I stumble upon?
I couldn't hear when they called my name,
Was I up with my game?
Wishes diminished in the rear of sky
I am left with a shadow dry,
One more season gets over,
Leaves me without a
sunny rainy shower.

It's Been a While

It's been a while to have watched a smile,
It's been a while to have crossed an isle.

In this place where I sit alone,
Neither they come nor do they leave me alone.

Hazardous hands of fate have crossed themselves,
If there were any mutiny of soul,
Perhaps, it waits for its role.

In the creeks of valley flows a tiny hope,
If there's a chance it could move up-slope.

It isn't in the nature to have me rise,
I don't say, it's a surmise.

It's been a while to have felt a rain,
It's been a while to have screamed in pain.

In this place where I am placed,
Neither a story is written nor erased.

The Shades of a Memory

They say it's never going to fade
Is it a colour or a shade?
Is it mingled in those
fervently thought thoughts?
Of you? Of us? Of those several
times of unspoken words?
Is it of life that met me on its way?
Or of lives I left untouched?
Is it of untraveled spaces?
Or of un-understood emotions?
It's imprinted right here,
Unseen, unknown
never to be heard,
never to be shown.

The Fissures of Fortune

A man walks behind me, intrigued,
His eyes, watch me in deference,
When I see him, his face charms me,
As if he wants to say something.

He asks my name,
As if to own it,
Name is all he can have after all,
Could he have more?
But for the fissures of the fortune!

I see him again, for one last time,
I remember the first time I had seen him,
And now I will see him only in past,
When we said adieus,
His eyes couldn't see me,
They just watched in emptiness.

Looking for You

If I could find you
I don't know what it'll feel like,
For now you aren't around
And I know how it feels.

Indescribable,
A fear has lived on inside me,
Undefined as a life we often live,
Fear too has an ageless desire to
Live.

As I live here without you,
The leaves of your memories sing,
And my desires for you are un-aged,
My hands await your touch,
Yet a fear unknown lives.

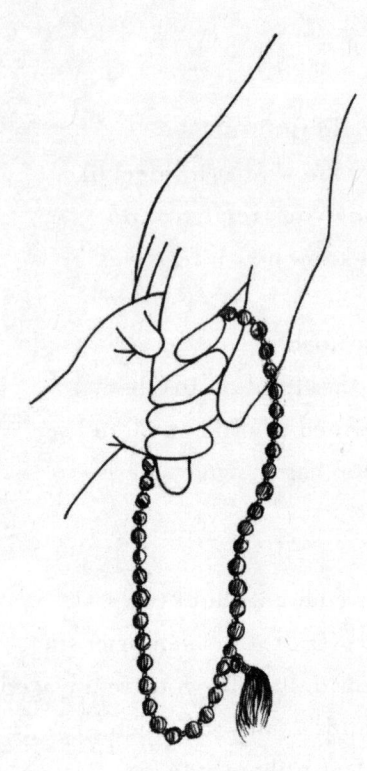

In Betrayal

Had it not for you,
I wouldn't have fallen so much.

Like a child's prayer, for long I held you close,
But with times we fell apart,
And long it has been since I felt you any near.

The passion for a union held me close,
A child saw you in the little big promises of his prayers,
Of his religion, where you weren't just a god.

A fickle human found me soon,
A child had lost you somewhere,
Or perhaps you got lost in the chaos you rule.

The flesh of belief lost its battle too soon,
Un-defeated in defeat I laid allegiance to none,
Still guilty of playing truant to my soul.

I withered like an autumn leave
and laid in a soiled existence, accused of
blasphemy to your rule.

Had it not for your betrayal,
I would have found a grave worthy somewhere,
But it ended for me without one.

The Notes of a Faithless

I write two notes of grief, one pink, one jaded,
What's in them to paint my soul?
The hyperbole of conviction leads me astray
to some pages of a prismed belief.

The writing is blemished, both for
the writer and the reader,
The inactive molecules of my existence jostle
to find their faith in the lines.

The pages shrink in size, timidly,
The time revels in this fruitless endeavour, yet again,
The restless hands briskly turn
to let go of the truth behind the words.

He Languishes

In the midnight of the dreams
a man endeavours to seek the earth
where soil of succour would touch his feet
and find him steady.

And as the dream awakes him into a new dawn,
the feet seem to be stuck in the same old soil,
Hard to abide with the law of the limits,
Whence will this murky existence let him go?

Perhaps, he is of a jaundiced soul,
Only suffering from the dreariness of his desires,
Unaccomplished in the day
what seems his own in the dim of light.

As this man brew himself new dreams tonight,
He wanders into grasslands of hope and
itinerates into an evergreen life,
Its real and majestic as hope is.

And then as the day sets out,
Once again he is gasping for a goal,
With eyes wide open
he struggles in a muddy field,
Unable to find his feet
he languishes once more in hopeless reveries.

Painted Dreams

Life seems to be running, hushing
the pace of dreams so cherished,
It's leaving me behind, far
farther than where I was ought to be.

The earth is unkind to my pace,
Life's so fragile too, such fragility
where wheels go bust
by mere friction of the earth.

As the painted dreams cover
the original scrambles, something vanishes in me,
When cast would be out, something pristine
would still be there, I believe.

I don't know if
paces could turn back,
Mired in a wire of destiny
all that's left is a sound of my first desire.

Nobody here cares to listen but for
empty dilapidated walls,
Hidden under layers of paint is a cherished
and faded colour, un-derived.

I am left behind in a race of men entrenched in glory,
What's left is one half of my dream, colourless,
long betrayed, and all that is mine
is as black as black.

The Beleaguered Tales

He comes to me and tells me a story,
Of a life lived in fear and lament,
A look at his face
and it reveals nothing that he speaks,
Or of anything he has endured.

He wears the long robes,
None that I could find here,
And the words are unknown too,
But story is a miracle
for the book of tales.

His voice trembles at the sound of a gun
but feet don't,
He sees the scars on his walls everyday,
Only he could see them,
And withstand too!

He belongs to the city of the kings,
Kings who rule the ruins,
The clouds of smoke envelope his home,
As he looks at the sky of smoke,
His eyes defy them, yet again.

Cacophony of a Muted Dream

The road seems muddy,
And mind is too timid,
Forlorn, a reality lives in the silent dorms,
Cacophony of dreams flourishes, albeit mute.

It's the reality of the chained humans,
Of the surgeons of the soul-less,
Green leaves don't heal here
like in older books.

They fall without noise and then
sudden sound of death creates a numb again,
Perhaps, they're waiting for the healers of a new order,
The new masters of their dreams.

The overwhelming majority of the men,
Where hands would find the succour,
And death would wane
in fear.

The motionless sky awaits that touch,
And blue day gleams with hope,
And yet,
A few stand far too away.

Never to be touched,
Never to be healed,
Never to succour in their freedom,
As they wait for their own.

In Memory of a Man

I think about a man, face forgotten,
But memories of his life are intact,
When he died I had wondered
If his closed eyes could feel anything.

I have often thought about the ones, who loved him,
Of those who will never see him again,
He is now a shadow in the woods for me,
Lamps lit in his memory for a while.

The ones whom he loved moved on, slowly,
They smiled back at life, for a while their life was
like a plundered village, robbed of love,
Their hands would rise in prayers
and their fingers shook as they rolled their beads of
     prayers.

He is now buried,
In his memory, his beloved goes and puts flowers on that
     place,
And weeps a little still,
All I wonder is if he is still sitting there cross-legged,
Like he always did.

Of Benefactors

It's a hall filled with men,
Men of various hue,
Hue unidentifiable by the eyes that see,
A few are fairer than others,
If only there was more to vision
than just seeing,
I could have seen more.

A man smiles at all,
Like he always does,
And a voice constantly speaks,
Of past
Of success
Of repeated glory.

Few men are rejoicing
in the generosity of their alms to the others,
And a man is handed a reward
Of his work,
From afar,
And he walks away.

He is humbled in his heart
by the shine of lights on his face,
He manages to hold his feet firm,

as he walks away,
obliged
to his benefactors.

The men of hue continue to talk,
The voice in the hall continues to speak,
The man humbled by the alms falters in his stride,
Yet finding his feet,
He goes to his place and claps for those
who didn't see him as he fell.

OF LOVE

*She weaves
a beautiful dream
of love,
She sits
clasping her memories
in her chest,
And sing them,
With every beat
of her heart.*

Of a Moon

The sky has few stars in it
and eyes little shine,
They see each other,
They talk
and they yearn.

They sit there,
They watch,
The moon is half
separated from the light it dwells on
and they pray.

The wind blows tonight
not so silently,
The darkness grows,
Their arms clasp
and they fear.

The sound of night gathers,
The horizons fade,
The sky is quiet
and their shadows merge
into one.

Love's Wine

If I ever ask you to be mine,
Perhaps you'll decline,
Of a horrid feeling that rejection carries,
I'll whine with swearing on some line.

I may sit on an edge of a roof,
Or find a worldly recline,
Just to forgive an unkind's design.

Uninhibited or stupefied,
I may again seek love's wine,
Lights fade, curtains fall,
Music doesn't fail this act divine.

Love's Feather

Love's feather was light,
It's touch heavy,
I let it fall free
upon me
to nest on my wings.

The spirit delighted
and my body enslaved,
In moments
I let it define me
into a muse.

Its place wasn't in me
but me,
Whispering in the rains
the droplets of its music
sung unto me.

With tender touch of love
its whiteness surrounded,
In shape of my dreams
love stared into my soul
and my heart beat to it.

You and I

Like million things
in the universe,
I know
You and I
exist in the moment
for a reason.

Like a star
who derives its light
from his beloved,
I breathe on
the prayers
of a soul.

I carry you
with me
like a river,
That flows along the shores
silently,
With million memories
afloat.

The shadows of doubt
of passing hours
cast them

once in a while,
To obliterate
the truth
of the heart.

The mind is a warrior,
It fights out
against me
each day
hopelessly,
Against a falling hope
of a union.

I knew it then
when you crossed
a distant land
to reach my hand
that I would survive,
To live a day
each day,
Only for you.

Your Light upon Me

The light that falls on my face reveals the truth,
It's hidden behind the softer creeks of the skin,
Though lost to many who had watched me instead,
Not for me, not for them, only for a sight.

It grows hazily upon me before it's quite clear,
I see it even in the darkest hours of the day,
The light doesn't always come in shine and sheen,
Or with million rays falling on your mortal being.

The light upon me is of calm words I hear from you,
The light which reveals me is your gentle softness,
This light is of your soul enshrined in goodness,
It is of million smiles you shower unhesitatingly for me.

Could you give me a hand to cross over to your universe?
Perhaps not, unlikely under these stars,
Yet your light shines on me, taking me into a dawn of my
    universe,
And all that glows on me tonight is your bequeath.

He Walks by Me

He walks by me with a smile,
Once again,
His eyes, as they fall on my meekly image
fill the emptiness of ages,
Un-aged I had waited for him
in lonely starlit nights,
Like a music of the flowing brook,
He had played on in my silence,
Like a sand of the desert I laid quiet
for the showers of his love,
An unkempt painting of a museum,
I had waited for his eyes to marvel me,
As he passes by like a prayer fulfilled
I speak with him in silence of our eyes.

Conjugal in Faith

They were two of them among the mortals,
Bounded by a dream resplendent,
Immersed in a truth only they knew,
Conjugal in faith and joined in fate.

When their hands felt their bodies,
They failed to grasp the timeless journey they had set on
where they would finally meet,
And those hands would feel eternity.
On way, the darkness had dared to devour their souls,
Light however filled the unfinished sketch of their love,
The rays penetrated far,
And darkness could not comprehend how transient she
    was.

The canvas of their reality drew a picture, poignant yet
    profound,
The multitude of colours filled their paces,
Unaware they kept on,
Only if they knew their Artist revels in kindness.

Love's Song

The music that plays reminds me of you,
When love was all just you,
When rhymes of your life defined my tunes,
When perspectives would yield to charming full moons,
Love wasn't hurt, it was the peace,
Love didn't rust; it was joy's precipice,
In the veins of heart, love's blood flew,
When I opened my eyes, you were my morning's view,
The starry nights were love's glow,
I saw your face in every rainbow,
I wonder, love stood to heal, where prayers were heard,
    without one to kneel,
Today in this quiet calm of evening,
Love seems so vague,
As unclear as city filled with haze,
Definitions have changed in a miraculous gaze,
All that's left is an inexplicable phrase.

Leaves Sing

Leaves sing happily
a song of joy
in a colour of green,
two birds,
a red, and a blue
sit amidst them.

They sit on a vine
of love
and kiss each other
sweet,
the wind cuddles their wings
to fly.

The birds in love
fill the song with their music,
the wind has a music too
that plays along,
and rainbow of colours
dances on the horizons.

The life
of the tree comes alive,
the earth seeks rain
for its bosom
and sky turns red
with beauty of their love.

I Search for You

I search for you,
On earth,
On waters,
In sky,
But I have not found you,
Not quite yet.

You wander
inside me sometimes
with a
prayer song
healing me
from within.

Sometimes you hide
in the darkness of
my thoughts
and you fear my shallowness
to drown you
in ignominy.

Sometimes you see me
quietly from the sides
lending me a voice
of my own.

To say the unspoken
with fearlessness.

Sometimes I endure
in silence
and in noise
the travails of destiny,
Never in a moment though have your
fortitude in me left my side.

Ode to Innocence

Come thy innocence, embrace me again,
Remember the sparrow with white feathers
who sat on rear wall of our home
in all her charming chirping ways.

We spent hours talking to her,
Glued to her eyes we saw a world beholden inside them,
It was the same wall besides the tree of neem
I once fell off and cried unbearably.

How we wished the shade of neem had fallen
more on our side of the wall,
The leaves of that tree were my fans in the summers
and hid us from the heat of the sun.

The strong branches we climbed in merry,
We were too tiny for those, yet you smiled
at our every climb, we fell off, rose up,
In love, in innocence, fearless.

We took vows together,
to never leave
each other,
howsoever much life may try to set us apart,
I remember you,

OF HER

She is a night of the sky,
An enormous star,
A moon in love,
A dream livid with black holes,
Spirit of her lovers soar higher with her glance,
She rises high,
She is a physics
that defies its laws.

Her Silence

Her silence plays into my mind like a tune,
And while the world goes past me silently,
She echoes,
She breathes into me,
And savours me gleefully.

I remember the touch of her hands,
Her deep voice rings in my ears
and devours my memory
like deep ocean waves that collide on the rocky shores
and drift away with splashes.

Her memory returns often, like rains,
I hail its arrival and the passage,
The fleeting moments recapitulate in joy,
And I know how she changed into me,
And how the solitude of a man was tormented.

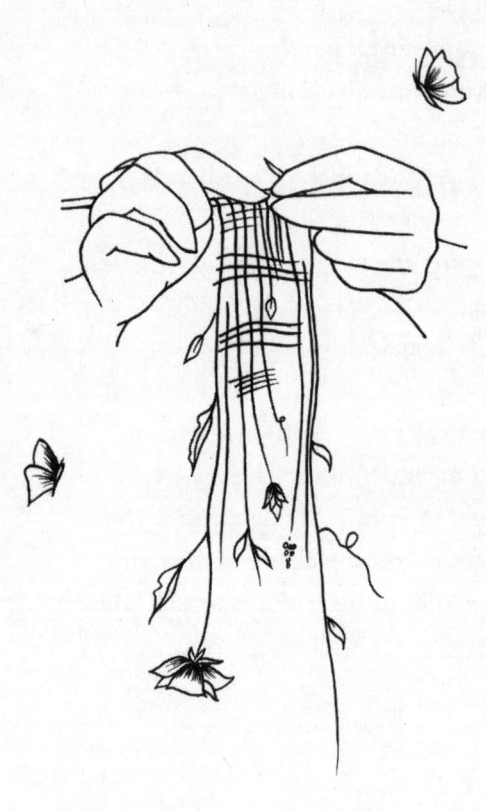

She Weaves a Cloth

She weaves a cloth for her body,
She is the maid of artistry,
And her mind, a reveller in colours
weaves a story into it.

The little threads stitch together,
Intricate patterns flow with her hands,
And a woven flower smiles with life
on a piece of rustic yarn.

A lighthearted boy plays near her,
The sounds of the scattered ware echo,
The smell of thick air fills her senses
as tiny droplets of sweat flow on her skin.

She lives in a hut of mud,
Poor, yet no sign of poverty,
Life abounds in her, surrounded with birds,
trees and
ponds of life, quietly she weaves.

She Sees Beauty

She sees beauty in things
and she walks amidst them,
She wanders in the nature's lap
and the quietitude of the world speaks to her.

She listens to the day's laughter
and to the night's music,
The solitude of the evening looks on
and the rhythm of life rejoices in her.

She looks at the simmering sun
and talks to the rising winds,
She walks to the empty horizons
and finds them near.

She sits in the old meadows
and listens to the sounds of ecstatic creatures,
They speak her heart's voice
and she knows they'll know her always.

I am a Bird

I am a bird,
I sing my song,
The song unfurls my wings, they delight,
My melody defines my flight,
I celebrate the joy,
I have celebrated the pain,
But never a note was sung in vain.

Eh, here he comes,
Says the song isn't blissful,
The blissful ah!
That woman, she just went through labour,
Am I to rejoice in her pain?
Am I to sing the notes that entertain?

My melody is old,
Stuck like sand on shores,
Millions endured it,
Speaks of hidden gold,
I live to delight my audience,
Can I deny them the salience?

I saw another bird,
Her wings got clipped,
The music got whipped,
And there is a lady bird,
Humming the painful notes of joy,
And I just sit quietly coy!

She Smiles

Lovely eyes they say,
And she looks away quietly,
The eyes that see the depth of love
and of agony
look around
to fathom measures of reality.

The hands are tender with pain,
Her palm lines are scattered,
Undeciphered,
Rough edges of life
lie there
without a story.

Her face, as fair as maiden
is empty of expressions,
The laughter
hides a story
untold,
Yet deeply felt.

And the smile is silent,
Stoically watching her moors,
Unconquered,
Yet given to faith,
She smiles
at life.

The Light of a Woman

Here she comes, that light again!
Here they still wander forlorn.

Dark is what she comes to shed
where they stay in an unknown dread.

Past the shadows of myth and lament
light caves through a narrow crescent.

Waltzed and exalted in a fool's faith
all they lay like a dead man's wreath.

Jostling with the midstream of channels of belief
weakened and played by a dark mischief.

The miserable shadows of the bygone
they are grayed stones and people neon.

Light doesn't waiver she marches on
to rescue belief into a new dawn.

A Broken Leaf

I wander on a lonely walk,
For all the talk among the trees,
I am a leaf broken, dead already.

The heat engulfs my brittle body,
Alas for life! All but pain is gone,
Light was life a while ago.

Now it's a hustler that pushes the demise,
If all is gone; why do I wander yet?
A lifeless leaf with a dead noise!

If I couldn't feel why the sun pinches me red?
If life were only to hold on to a branch,
Why does a thought of life linger in me?

Why does wind play on my fragile body?
And why does she cajole me to lay silent?
And why do they still burn me to death?

Is It Mine?

They say,
And I obey,
It's forbidden to walk in the light,
So I bear the darkness's fright.

They lend me a voice,
Is it mine?
Or theirs?
Or is it everyone's
who is frolicking with the divine?
My tongue shivers,
Momentarily I flail,
And yet again I fail.

They want me to rise,
Beyond the tiny prize,
I stand,
I speak,
To say something,
To them?
Or to their lords?
Or to their darkness's end?
And I just pretend.

They want me to see
the destiny's play,
I watch,
I hear,
And I say,
It reeks of pain,
Justice inhumane,
I want to change
the way histories arrange,
They are quiet
and I fight.

She Wears a Thin Smile

It's quite late to search for the messiahs,
In the world of the sinews and bubbles,
When I look at her,
She wears a thin smile,
Look close, those cheeks are red,
Of blush or pain?

I hold her hands,
The lines are dark on hardened hands,
She whisks me away, asks me to stay quiet,
Couldn't I look beyond the visible lines?

She watches me fold my hands around her,
Does she say anything?
Is she quietly timid in the fold?
Or her wishes got a life?
I won't know, just like she won't.

Is there a stain to identity?
Or to just exist?
And I am here
vouching for her,
In piety or belief?

Her voice is as slender
as rain on the grass
falling gently on earth,
In my story seldom did she cry,
When they took her away,
She just uttered a word,
A word, I couldn't hear.

Forever My Credence

Didn't you owe me for your vice?
A dime they say is a worthy price!
But million lives wouldn't suffice,
For when you rolled me like a dice!

Were I a bet with a name?
Or did you lose me in a man's game?
The generous king could be so lame!
Perhaps, you didn't know the strength of a dame!

The group of wise stayed quiet,
While the rules were written all in white!
Centuries couldn't forgive the silence,
And the war cry is forever my credence!

In a Woman Like You

In a woman like you,
And I sense a dTWejTha vu,
Could they unveil a tale?
Of a woman who is frail.

While I see you, I see a face,
Undeterred but delectable to eyes,
You carry unguarded expressions of faith,
A man moves, he looks at you,
And all you do is stare back, unmoved.

Let's see what he sees in you,
A shade of life or a joyful sight,
Or a moment of guile,
To fritter away his while.

And as you watch it all,
Near the shade of an old tree,
A man finds his reflection in you,
And a story unveils,
Perhaps, this time it belongs to you.

The Girl Stands

This girl stands here, her head is covered
with a torned piece of cloth,
She consumes heat of the raging sun with deep breaths,
She did look for some shade, but had found none.

A man comes and stands near her,
She looks at his face and then turns away,
She knows the rules she needs to obey,
Deep inside, though, she makes a conversation with this
    stranger.

Silently, she plays out her smile and her
rhythmic nods,
She imagines a different place,
On a fairytale itinerary with the stranger.

But she knows she can't smile,
She also knows how to hide it, her head moves away,
She rearranges the head-cover once again,
She wants to smile even if he doesn't smile back.

But this stranger is unlike others,
He wants to talk to this girl in sun,
Her simple beauty enchants him truly,
He asks her something,

The girl faintly looks up at the face so vibrant.

She listens too but her nods don't play out as she had
    imagined,
There are stares staring her as they always have,
She doesn't say anything; she had so much to say,
The man now walks away,
She thinks if he could stay for a while longer.

Silently, she stays silent,
She has lost a string she could have found,
Perhaps she knew it all along,
The sun still shines and she is standing there still,
Her head is half covered, waiting.

A Birth Unwanted

I watch a girl sit barefoot
I look close,
She isn't just another face or is she?
She isn't the only one barefoot I have seen though,
Is she just another harrowed breath of life?
A vision we never dream of.

It's a face that carries silent screams,
A face of nothingness in abundance,
The feet are impatient yet bounded in helpless patience,
Was a smile meant for her?
Was a dream due to her?

She is a young face creased with age,
Does she have a name?
Is she born of silent desires or unwanted blessings?
She is a prayer in silence and a thought never to be.

Did the womb of her birth matter?
She is conceived of pain
Not of her,
But of the eyes who never saw her.

A Leaf of Fall

She falls without a noise,
With no desire to live again,
She is a leaf of fall.

Yet she is beautiful
to the lovers
who pass her by.

They feel her presence
in the sound of their feet
and in the yellowness of her being.

She offers no love,
No grief,
She is a leaf of fall.

She Walks Alone

She is listening
to them, as she walks
alone,
Her fears speak to her
with a deafening noise,
And create a stir in her walk.

They look at her bare feet
and her bare skin,
The neck that attracts!
The asking stare!
She wants to cover them
with shame, but how?

Those eyes tease her
and she remembers a story,
Of the robes that were torn,
in the midst of kings,
Would those be enough to cover her?
Or to cover those eyes?
Of the kings and slaves alike.

She quivers!
She is scared of the death,
Of the tyranny
of the questions
upon her coffin,
Of her frivolity
to walk free, among men!

Of Different Women

I grew up to be quaint,
Normal wasn't my norm,
And I didn't know it was
till I saw they needed a normal
everyday.

I haven't given up on me yet,
They have,
Their normal doesn't suit mine,
And do I care?
I don't think so.

They want me to walk
Like they do,
They want me to talk
Like they do,
They even want a smile similar,
And every time they smile!

And I defy that,
I can't smile a stale smile,
I can't mimic a walk or a talk,
I am my own,
And I have always been.

Of Joyful Cage

She lives in a joyful cage,
The men admire her,
And the women envy,
For she is the beautiful damsel
of this land.

And her thoughts move
not beyond herself,
Constrained to impress those
who adore her
and torment those who rival.

She sees beauty
in a beautiful silk
wrapped on her,
And the soul is hidden
below the softness of the silk.

Like everything transient
they weren't forever,
She hadn't searched for herself,
Her without them,
And she trembles in fear.

She searches for a face,
The one she admired much
and it has withered,
She moans, not aware yet
of the spirit un-aged.

Of Subjugation

They asked her for the will
to submit the only soul she had,
Isn't it much to ask for?
Or is it just the endeavour of the soulless
to wish to peep into the mercies of her gods.

Too hard to believe that they lie there in plenty,
Her demons of sorrow would want to share,
But with whom?
Waving on the cliff of despair,
Her hands pain to leave the scars behind.

She is Silent, Forevermore

She looks at me often,
Maybe at my misfortune,
Maybe at her lost hopes,
And maybe that's her solace,
And she looks on, solemnly.

She wanted me near her,
In all her glories, in all her failures,
In the precious hours of laughter,
And it wasn't destined to be,
And she laments, relentlessly.

She was the bearer of my faith,
She wanted the time to release me
from the chained path I chose,
She doesn't know how I grew faithless,
And she is in pain, perpetually.

She knows how distant I grew,
How faintly I remember love,
She doesn't talk anymore
of that splendid dream she wove,
And she is silent, forevermore.

Of Dreams of Freedom

A girl wishes to change the world,
She goes to the fields
and gathers a few like her,
She makes a union
of free girls.

She speaks voluminously
of how she was incarcerated
by the ideals
of an ordinary life
and now she is free
and they all say in one.

They go to the fields
where girls like them sow the grains
for a good harvest
to feed their families,
And still they carry jaundiced eyes
and half-fed stomachs.

She takes them on a journey
towards a modern school
where all are singing and playing
in bright blue skirts and beautiful braids,
They stand near the wall

and watch them in wonder.
They want to go to this school,
They go to the guard to let them in,
And the guard says dearies,
'You don't have a place here'
Needs money to get admission,
And they decide to work for it.

And go back to the fields,
To earn for themselves,
For their freedom,
Their union stands,
Their goals unfulfilled,
Their dream remains.

To a Father, from Daughter

I wouldn't know the sound of music
if it weren't for those tunes
of yesterday,
When you played them near me
with devotion.

I wouldn't know the whispers of truth
if it weren't for your story
of how a penny turned into gold
with a man's hands
in the toil.

I wouldn't know the warmth of love
if it weren't for your heart,
What it knew without knowing,
What love's faith could find
without seeing.

I wouldn't know the compassion
if it weren't for your soul's prowess
to inflict relief to the pain
of a dying man
with a prayer.

5